Child poverty in the developing world

David Gordon, Shailen Nandy, Christina Pantazis,
Simon Pemberton and Peter Townsend

First published in Great Britain in October 2003 by

The Policy Press
Fourth Floor
Beacon House
Queen's Road
Bristol BS8 1QU
UK

Tel +44 (0)117 331 4054
Fax +44 (0)117 331 4093
e-mail tpp-info@bristol.ac.uk
www.policypress.org.uk

British Library Cataloguing in Publication Data

A catalogue record for this book is available from the British Library

ISBN 1 86134 559 3 paperback

David Gordon is Professor of Social Justice, **Shailen Nandy** is a Research Associate, **Christina Pantazis** is a Research Fellow, **Simon Pemberton** is a Post-Doctoral Research Fellow, all at the School for Policy Studies, University of Bristol. **Peter Townsend** is Professor of International Social Policy at the London School of Economics and Political Science.

Funding for this study and publication was provided by UNICEF.

The views expressed in this report are those of the authors and do not necessarily represent the views of UNICEF or its Division of Policy and Planning.

Cover design by Qube Design Associates, Bristol.
Front cover: photograph kindly supplied by Panos Pictures © Paul Weinberg.
Printed and bound in Great Britain by Hobbs the Printers Ltd, Southampton.

Contents

List of tables and figures

Tables

Figures

Acknowledgements

The authors wish to express their thanks to UNICEF for providing a grant which funded two stages of research developed from 2000, involving collaborative work between the University of Bristol and the London School of Economics and Political Science. In a succession of meetings with UNICEF staff and, in particular, with Alberto Minujin, at meetings in London, Rio de Janeiro and New York, the plan described in these pages evolved and was agreed. The idea for the work sprang from the new focus on children *themselves* rather than on families and communities in general that was reflected in UNICEF's programme during the 1990s.

The first priority was to review direct and indirect information about children and to find the strengths and weaknesses of existing data about children's conditions and needs. While a great deal of national and international research on Articles in the Convention on the Rights of the Child has been completed, the relationship between child poverty and child rights had not been fully explored. Thanks are due to Jo Beall, Jonathan Bradshaw, Meghnad Desai and David Piachaud, John Micklewright, Giovanni Andrea Cornia and Jane Falkingham for the ideas being developed and especially the comparative studies on the transition countries of Eastern Europe published by the Innocenti Research Centre in Florence, Italy. The valuable assistance, in the early weeks, of Ceema Namazie in reviewing child data in Kyrgyz is gratefully acknowledged. We would also like to thank Enrique Delamonica and Bill O'Neil for their very helpful comments on the first draft. Jan Vandemoortele also provided us with considerable help, support and encouragement. The establishment of the Centre for the Study of Human Rights at the London School of Economics and Political Science (LSE) has been a source of inspiration during the period of the research and, in particular, Christine Chinkin and the first Director of the Centre, Conor Gearty, have argued through ideas relevant to the research.

Several classes of postgraduate students at both the University of Bristol, Birmingham University and LSE have generated a stimulating debate on the measurement of child poverty in developing countries.

The DHS data were provided by MACRO International whose staff were extremely helpful and gave us a great deal of assistance.

The dependable advice and support of Jean Corston and Helen Gordon throughout this project is also warmly acknowledged.

Child poverty and child rights in developing countries

This short report presents the first ever scientific measurement of the extent and depth of child poverty in all the developing regions of the world. It represents a summary of a much larger research report on child poverty and child rights funded by the United Nations Children's Fund (UNICEF) (Gordon et al, 2001, 2003). Full details of this research will be published in a future book on this subject.

This measurement of child poverty is based on internationally agreed definitions arising from the international framework of child rights. In successive annual reports, UNICEF has argued that poverty is one of the greatest obstacles to the survival and development of children. The near-consensus reached by all national governments in framing the 1989 Convention on the Rights of the Child gave momentum to serious and effective work to reduce violations of a number of rights relevant to the reduction of child poverty in different countries.

Poverty denies children their fundamental human rights. Severe or extreme poverty can cause children permanent damage – both physically and mentally – stunt and distort their development and destroy opportunities of fulfilment, including the roles they are expected to play successively as they get older in family, community and society. Both research and administrative data show that investment in basic social services for children is a key element to ensure success in alleviating their poverty. It also shows that a minimal level of family resources to enable parents to meet the needs of their children are required – even when families are prepared to put their own needs or the needs of work and other social claims on them in second place. If there are insufficient resources to satisfy children's needs – however hard parents can be shown to try – then this can cause other obligations and relationships to crumble. This is why UNICEF insists that "poverty reduction begins with children".

The World Declaration and Plan of Action adopted by the World Summit for Children in 1990 set forth a vision of a 'first call' for children by establishing seven major and 20 supporting goals that were quantifiable and considered achievable by 2000.

UNICEF has reported on progress towards these goals[1]. In 2000, it was found that some of the trends in the 1980s and 1990s had deepened rather than lifted public concern. Since 1987, the number of people in developing countries, other than in East Asia and the Pacific, with less than $1 a day, had increased by 12 million a year. In many countries, the extreme poor had been "left further behind". And "the evidence is compelling that the 1990s saw a widening in the gap between rich and poor countries as well as between rich and poor people within countries, both in terms of incomes and social outcomes" (UNICEF, 2000, pp 9, 17, 45).

In a statement prepared for the end-of-the-decade review, planned for September 2001 but postponed until May 2002, the Executive Director of UNICEF,

---

[1] In 2000, an exhaustive and exacting end-of-decade review of progress towards the Summit goals was undertaken, drawing on a range of sources not previously available, from data collected in the Multiple Indicator Cluster Surveys (MICS), the Demographic and Health Surveys (DHS) and national progress reports from nearly 150 countries (UNICEF, 2002a).

Carol Bellamy, was obliged to call attention to the "mixture of conspicuous achievement and dispiriting failure" for children. Most governments had not lived up to the promises made at the 1990 World Summit for Children. Despite some progress, stronger leadership and more sustained policies were required (UNICEF, 2002b).

At the UN General Assembly's Special Session on Children in September 2002, the latest information was debated. The 10 years since the 1990 World Summit for Children were found to have yielded mixed results. Three million fewer children under the age of five now died each year, due in large part to immunisation programmes and the dedicated efforts of families and communities. In developing countries, 28 million fewer children under the age of five suffered the debilitating effects of malnutrition. More than 175 countries were polio-free and 104 had eliminated neonatal tetanus. Yet, despite these gains, more than 10 million children still died each year from mostly preventable diseases – 150 million were estimated to be malnourished, some 600 million children still lived in poverty and more than 100 million – the majority of them girls – were not in school. The number of children orphaned by AIDS had grown from 1.2 million to 10.4 million and under-five mortality from AIDS was expected to double by the year 2010 (UN, 2002 and see also UNICEF, 2002c).

UNICEF has strengthened its work on poverty. It has actively participated in international conferences and government exchanges and published documents and promoted policies – many aimed at reducing child poverty. Its report, *Poverty reduction begins with children* (UNICEF, 2000), was of prime concern at the special session of the UN General Assembly in Geneva in June 2000. The reports from the UNICEF Innocenti Research Centre cover a wide range of research into child rights and development in both rich and poor countries, especially that affecting child poverty, including, for example, *A league table of child poverty in rich nations* (UNICEF Innocenti Research Centre, 2000), and extensive work on poverty in the transition economies and on the problems of child labour in India, Sub-Saharan Africa and Latin America, and the ramifying problems of children caught up in armed conflict.

The authors of this report seek to contribute to the consolidation and extension of this work to include all the developing regions of the world.

Measurement of child poverty and standard of living

Introduction

This chapter will present a very brief summary of recent research on the international comparative measurement of child poverty.

The 21st century world is one in which a vast quantity of information on all aspects of human existence is easily available, often via the Internet. The 1990s witnessed a revolution in the collection of high quality statistical information about the world's children and their families. A range of harmonised survey instruments, such as the Living Standards and Measurement Surveys (LSMS), the Demographic and Health Surveys (DHS) and the Multiple Indicator Cluster Surveys (MICS) have been used successfully in a large number of countries (see Gordon et al, 2001, 2003, for discussion). However, despite these advances and increasing concern about the issue of child poverty, there are still few analyses of the standard of living and well-being of children in developing countries. In fact, there is a surprising lack of direct information on children per se. With the notable exception of basic health and education statistics, much of the statistical information on 'children' is derived from measures of the situation of the child's family or main carer. Children are routinely considered as a property of their household and are assumed to share equally in its fortunes (or misfortunes).

Income and child poverty

One of the most commonly used international indicators of 'poverty' for both adults and children is the per capita Gross Domestic Product (GDP) – or Gross National Product (GNP) – of a country. Numerous studies use these kinds of economic activity indicators as a proxy for poverty (for example, Sachs et al, 2001). Although it can be expected that the distribution of child poverty would broadly conform with the global distribution of GDP per head, this is a very crude way in which to measure and map child poverty. These kinds of economic statistics, derived from national accounts data, are only proxy measures of the social situation and living conditions within a country, and it must be remembered that there are large disparities in both income and living conditions *within* most countries as well as *between* them. It was inherent inadequacies of these kinds of analysis that led to the growth of the social indicators movement in the 1960s (Bauer, 1966).

The revolution in volume, coverage and quality of household survey data that occurred in the 1990s has recently allowed the analysis of income data on a global scale based on the directly measured income of households, rather than on their inferred incomes from national accounts (Milanovic, 2002). Analyses are so far available for both 1988 and 1993 and data for later years are currently being assembled. It would be possible to use the global household level income data from social surveys collected by Milanovic and his co-workers to produce a low income 'poverty' analysis for households with children for the regions of the world. For example, a similar type of analysis to the World Bank's $1 per day poverty line could be used, based on income rather than expenditure/consumption. There are, however, a number of reasons why this kind of approach to measuring child poverty in developing countries is far from ideal (see Gordon et al, 2001, for discussion).

- Little is known about the income/expenditure/ consumption needs of children in most developing countries and how these needs may vary by age, gender and location. Therefore, any income or expenditure/consumption poverty threshold for children would have to be set at an essentially arbitrary level given the current lack of knowledge about children's needs. In particular, the World Bank's (1990) consumption-based poverty definition in terms of *the expenditure necessary to buy a minimum standard of nutrition* is inappropriate for measuring child poverty, particularly for young children who have low food requirements but numerous additional basic needs that require expenditure. Many academic commentators have severely criticised the World Bank's $1 per day poverty threshold for not being an adequate definition of adults' needs in developing countries (for example, Comparative Research Programme on Poverty, 2001). Therefore, setting an arbitrary child poverty income threshold is unjustifiable and would be likely to lead to incorrect policy conclusions.
- Household-based income and expenditure/ consumption 'poverty' analyses usually assume an equal sharing of resources within a household. This assumption is unlikely to be correct for many 'poor' and 'rich' households with children. In 'poor' families across the world, parents often sacrifice their own needs in order to ensure that their children can have some of the things they need (that is, children are often allocated a disproportionate share of household resources). Conversely, in 'rich' households parents may spend less than expected on young children so as not to 'spoil' them.
- There are many technical problems involved in using either an income or expenditure/ consumption approach to measuring child poverty in developing countries, for example, calculating equivalent spending power of national currencies using purchasing power parity, equivalisation by household type, controlling for infrequent, irregular or seasonal purchases, under-reporting bias and other measurement errors, data discontinuities, quantifying the benefits from

'home' production and the use of durables, and so on (for a discussion of these issues, see Atkinson, 1990; Goodman and Webb, 1995; Reddy and Pogge, 2002).
- The extent of child poverty is not just dependent on family income but also on the availability of infrastructure and services, such as health, education and water supply.
- Internationally agreed definitions of poverty are all concerned with outcomes (for example, the effects of the lack of command over resources over time).

International definitions of poverty

Poverty, like evolution or health, is both a scientific and a moral concept. Many of the problems of measuring poverty arise because the moral and scientific concepts are often confused. In scientific terms, a child or their household is 'poor' when they have both a low standard of living and a lack of resources over time (often measured in terms of low income). In many circumstances, a child or their household would not be considered to be 'poor' if they have a low income but a reasonable standard of living (although they are likely to be at risk of becoming 'poor').

A low standard of living is often measured by using deprivation indicators (high deprivation equals a low standard of living) or by consumption expenditure (low consumption expenditure equals a low standard of living). Of these two methods, deprivation indices are more accurate since consumption expenditure is often only measured over a brief period and is obviously not independent of income currently available. Deprivation indices are broader measures because they reflect different aspects of living standards, including personal, physical and mental conditions, local and environmental facilities, social activities and customs.

For scientific purposes, broad measures of both income and standard of living are desirable. When the definition of income is extended operationally to include the value of assets and receipt of goods and services in kind, the correlation between the two becomes greater (see Townsend, 1979, p 1176). Standards of living comprise varied elements, including both the material and social conditions in which children and their families live and their participation in the social, cultural, economic and political life of their country.

A wide range of different methods have been used by governments and academic researchers to measure poverty and the merits and problems of each method have been classified and discussed by the Comparative Research Programme on Poverty (CROP) of the International Social Science Council (Øyen et al, 1996) and, more recently, by Boltvinik (1999) on behalf of the UN Development Programme.

Social science research has shown that all cultures have a concept and definition of poverty although these definitions often vary (Gordon and Spicker, 1998). A major problem with many previous attempts to measure poverty on a global scale is that there was no agreed definition of poverty. This situation changed at the World Summit for Social Development in Copenhagen (UN, 1995). Among the innovations agreed in the 1995 *Copenhagen declaration and programme of action* was the preparation of national anti-poverty plans based on measures in all countries of 'absolute' and 'overall' poverty. The aim was to link – if not reconcile – the difference between industrialised and developing world conceptions, allow more reliable comparisons to be made between countries and regions and to make easier the identification of acceptable priorities for action. In developing anti-poverty strategies, the international agreement at Copenhagen was a breakthrough and the governments of 117 countries agreed to these definitions of absolute and overall poverty.

Absolute poverty is defined as:

> ... a condition characterised by severe deprivation of basic human needs, including food, safe drinking water, sanitation facilities, health, shelter, education and information. It depends not only on income but also on access to social services.

Overall poverty takes various forms, including:

> ... lack of income and productive resources to ensure sustainable livelihoods; hunger and malnutrition; ill health; limited or lack of access to education and other basic services; increased morbidity and mortality from illness; homelessness and inadequate housing; unsafe environments and social

discrimination and exclusion. It is also characterised by lack of participation in decision-making and in civil, social and cultural life. It occurs in all countries: as mass poverty in many developing countries, pockets of poverty amid wealth in developed countries, loss of livelihoods as a result of economic recession, sudden poverty as a result of disaster or conflict, the poverty of low-wage workers, and the utter destitution of people who fall outside family support systems, social institutions and safety nets.

> Women bear a disproportionate burden of poverty and children growing up in poverty are often permanently disadvantaged. Older people, people with disabilities, indigenous people, refugees and internally displaced persons are also particularly vulnerable to poverty. Furthermore, poverty in its various forms represents a barrier to communication and access to services, as well as a major health risk, and people living in poverty are particularly vulnerable to the consequences of disasters and conflicts.

After the Copenhagen Summit, the UN established four task forces to prepare coordinated action on the major commitments from all the global summits, including children, women, population, habitat and social development. The conclusion of this work was a statement of commitment to action to eradicate poverty issued in June 1998 by the executive heads of all UN agencies (Langmore, 2000). Poverty eradication "is the key international commitment and a central objective of the United Nations system".

Poverty was described as:

> Fundamentally, poverty is a denial of choices and opportunities, a violation of human dignity. It means lack of basic capacity to participate effectively in society. It means not having enough to feed and cloth a family, not having a school or clinic to go to, not having the land on which to grow one's food or a job to earn one's living, not having access to credit. It means insecurity, powerlessness and exclusion of individuals, households and communities. It means susceptibility to violence, and it often implies living on marginal or fragile environments, without access to clean water or sanitation. (UN Economic and Social Council, 1998)

Income is important but access to public goods – safe water supply, roads, healthcare, education – is of equal or greater importance, particularly in developing countries. These are the views of both the governments of the world and the institutions of the UN, and poverty measurement clearly needs to respond to these views.

There is a need to look beyond income and consumption expenditure poverty measures and at both the effects of low family income on children and the effects of inadequate service provision for children (Mehrotra et al, 2000; Vandemoortele, 2000). It is a lack of investment in good quality education, health and other public services in many parts of the world that is as significant a cause of child poverty as low family incomes. Nobel Laureate, Amartya Sen, has argued that, in developing countries, poverty is best measured directly using indicators of standard of living rather than indirectly using income or consumption measures:

> In an obvious sense the direct method is superior to the income method ... it could be argued that only in the absence of direct information regarding the satisfaction of the specified needs can there be a case for bringing in the intermediary of income, so that the income method is at most a second best. (Sen, 1981)

Furthermore, Atkinson (1990) has argued that:

> The definition of the poverty indicator, of the poverty level, and of the unit of analysis are not purely technical matters. They involve judgements about the objectives of policy. Any cross-country comparison of poverty has therefore to consider the purposes of this analysis and the relationship between these objectives and those pursued within the countries studied.

Measuring child poverty in developing countries

The purpose of the research detailed in this report was to produce the first accurate and reliable measure of the extent and severity of child poverty in the developing world using internationally agreed definitions of poverty. In particular, the primary

objective was to produce an operational measure of absolute poverty for children as agreed at the World Summit for Social Development.

The governments of 117 countries agreed that absolute poverty is "a condition characterised by severe deprivation of basic human needs" (UN, 1995). Brown and Madge (1982), in their major review of over 100 years of literature on deprivation, argued that:

> Deprivations are loosely regarded as unsatisfactory and undesirable circumstances, whether material, emotional, physical or behavioural, as recognised by a fair degree of societal consensus. Deprivations involve a lack of something generally held to be desirable – an adequate income, good health, etc – a lack which is associated to a greater or lesser extent with some degree of suffering.

Similarly, Townsend (1987) has argued that:

> Deprivation may be defined as a state of observable and demonstrable disadvantage relative to the local community or the wider society or nation to which an individual, family or group belongs. The idea has come to be applied to conditions (that is, physical, emotional or social states or circumstances) rather than resources and to specific and not only general circumstances, and therefore can be distinguished from the concept of poverty.

The two concepts of poverty and deprivation are tightly linked but there is general agreement that the concept of deprivation covers the various conditions, independent of income, experienced by people who are poor, while the concept of poverty refers to the lack of income and other resources which make those conditions inescapable or at least highly likely.

Deprivation can be conceptualised as a continuum that ranges from no deprivation, through mild, moderate and severe deprivation to extreme deprivation at the end of the scale (Gordon, 2002). Figure 2.1 illustrates this concept.

Figure 2.1: Continuum of deprivation

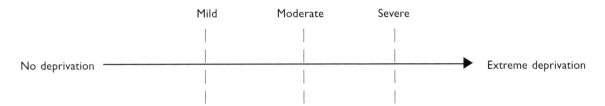

In order to measure absolute poverty among children, it is necessary to define the threshold measures of severe deprivation of basic human need for:

- food
- safe drinking water
- sanitation facilities
- health
- shelter
- education
- information
- access to services.

A taxonomy of severe deprivation is required, since a reliable taxonomy is a prerequisite for any scientific measurement. In this research, the threshold measures for severe deprivation, as far as is practicable, conform to internationally agreed standards and conventions. Theoretically, we have defined 'severe deprivation of basic human need' as those circumstances that are highly likely to have serious adverse consequences for the health, well-being and development of children. Severe deprivations are causally related to 'poor' developmental outcomes both long and short term. Table 2.1 shows the idealised operational definitions of deprivation for the eight criteria in the World Summit definition of absolute poverty (from Gordon et al, 2001).

Operational measures of absolute poverty for children

The most appropriate available data which could be used to operationalise the measurement of child poverty in developing countries were the DHS and, for China, the China Health and Nutrition Surveys. High quality household and individual survey data were available from 46 countries, collected since the

1990s (and, for most countries, much more recently – see Gordon et al, 2001). Detailed face-to-face interview data were available for almost 500,000 households, of which over 380,000 were households with children (Table 2.2). The total number of children in this aggregated sample was nearly 1.2 million (approximately one in every 1,500 children in the developing world) and the information about the children's lives was reported by their mothers or main carers. This is probably the largest and most accurate survey sample of children ever assembled. It is a particularly good sample of African children (with interview data on one child in every 650) although the number of children in the East Asian and Pacific sample (123,400) represents a lower sampling fraction (one child in every 4,500).

It was not possible to use the survey data to operationalise the idealised definitions of severe deprivation of basic human need that we had established prior to the data analysis phase of this research (see Table 2.1). Some compromise always has to be made when dealing with survey data. However, the severe deprivation measures that were available are conceptually very close to our idealised measures. The measures used were[2]:

1) *Severe food deprivation:* children whose heights and weights for their age were more than −3 standard deviations below the median of the international reference population, that is, severe anthropometric failure.

2) *Severe water deprivation:* children who only had access to surface water (for example, rivers) for drinking or who lived in households where the nearest source of water was more than 15 minutes away (indicators of severe deprivation of water quality or quantity).

---

[2]   Full technical details on how all these measures were constructed can be found in Gordon et al (2003).

Table 2.1: Operational definitions of deprivation for children

Deprivation	Mild	Moderate	Severe	Extreme
Food	Bland diet of poor nutritional value	Going hungry on occasion	Malnutrition	Starvation
Safe drinking water	Not having enough water on occasion due to lack of sufficient money	No access to water in dwelling but communal piped water available within 200m of dwelling or less than 15 minutes walk away	Long walk to water source (more than 200m or longer than 15 minutes). Unsafe drinking water (eg open water)	No access to water
Sanitation facilities	Having to share facilities with another household	Sanitation facilities outside dwelling	No sanitation facilities in or near dwelling	No access to sanitation facilities
Health	Occasional lack of access to medical care due to insufficient money	Inadequate medical care	No immunisation against diseases. Only limited non-professional medical care available when sick	No medical care
Shelter	Dwelling in poor repair. More than 1 person per room	Few facilities in dwelling, lack of heating, structural problems. More than 3 people per room	No facilities in house, non-permanent structure, no privacy, no flooring, just one or two rooms. More than 5 people per room	Roofless – no shelter
Education	Inadequate teaching due to lack of resources	Unable to attend secondary but can attend primary education	Child is 7 or older and has received no primary or secondary education	Prevented from learning due to persecution and prejudice
Information	Cannot afford newspapers or books	No television but can afford a radio	No access to radio, television or books or newspapers	Prevented from gaining access to information by government, etc
Basic social services	Health and education facilities available but occasionally of low standard	Inadequate health and education facilities near by (eg less than 1 hour travel)	Limited health and education facilities a day's travel away	No access to health or education facilities

3) *Severe deprivation of sanitation facilities:* children who had no access to a toilet of any kind in the vicinity of their dwelling, that is, no private or communal toilets or latrines.

4) *Severe health deprivation:* children who had not been immunised against any diseases or young children who had a recent illness involving diarrhoea and had not received any medical advice or treatment.

5) *Severe shelter deprivation:* children in dwellings with more than five people per room (severe overcrowding) or with no flooring material (for example, a mud floor).

6) *Severe educational deprivation:* children aged between 7 and 18 who had never been to school and were not currently attending school (no professional education of any kind).

7) *Severe information deprivation:* children aged between 3 and 18 with no access to radio, television, telephone or newspapers at home.

8) *Severe deprivation of access to basic services:* children living 20km or more from any type of school or 50km or more from any medical facility with doctors. Unfortunately, this kind of information was only available for a few countries, so it has not been possible to construct accurate regional estimates of severe deprivation of access to basic services.

Children who suffer from these levels of severe deprivation are very likely to be living in absolute poverty because, in the overwhelming majority of cases, the cause of severe deprivation of basic human need is invariably a result of lack of resources/ income. However, there may also be some children in this situation due to discrimination (for example, girls suffering severe education deprivation) or due to disease (severe malnutrition can be caused by some diseases). For this reason, we have assumed that a

Table 2.2: Summary sample size details, by region

Region	Sample size (all households)	Number of households with children	Number of children in sample	Number of children under 18 (UN figures, 2000)
Latin America and Caribbean	95,963	71,863	189,709	193,482,000
South Asia	116,443	95,960	276,609	603,761,000
Middle East and North Africa	34,980	28,432	106,280	154,037,000
Sub-Saharan Africa	178,056	142,494	487,885	317,860,000
East Asia and Pacific	62,773	49,858	123,400	559,615,000
World total	488,215	388,607	1,183,883	1,828,755,000

child is living in absolute poverty *only* if he or she suffers from two or more severe deprivations of basic human need as defined above.

The main practical criteria used to select these measures of severe deprivations were:

- data availability for a large number of children;
- the definitions must be consistent with international norms and agreements.

The purpose of this study was to measure children's living conditions that were so severely deprived that they were indicative of absolute poverty. Thus, the measures used represent more severe deprivations than the indicators frequently published by international organisations. For example, 'no schooling' instead of 'non-completion of primary school', 'no sanitations facilities' instead of 'unimproved sanitations facilities', 'no immunisations of any kind' instead of 'incomplete immunisation against common diseases', 'malnutrition measured as anthropometric failure below −3 standard deviations from the reference population median' instead of 'below −2 standard deviations from the reference median', and so on. We have, in the tradition of Rowntree (1901), tried to err on the side of caution in defining these indicators of absolute poverty in such severe terms that few would question that these living conditions were unacceptable.

3

Absolute poverty and severe deprivation among children in the developing world

Introduction

This chapter describes the distribution of severe deprivation of basic human need among children in the developing world. It begins by summarising the main results of the study and is followed by three sub-sections which each consider the data in more detail. The first of these sub-sections compares the extent of severe deprivation in the regions of the developing world with regards to each of the seven indicators, that is, food, water, sanitation, health, shelter, education and access to information. Differences within regions are also examined in terms of gender and locality. The second sub-section examines the distribution of severe deprivation, defined in terms of children experiencing one or more severe deprivations. The third and final sub-section compares absolute poverty rates between and within regions – where absolute poverty is defined as the condition of those children who suffer from multiple severe deprivations – two or more different types of severe deprivation of basic human need (see Chapter 2 for discussion).

Summary of main results on absolute poverty

- Over a third of all children in developing countries (37% or 674 million) are living in absolute poverty. This is a shocking result given that absolute poverty has been defined in this study as suffering from two or more forms of severe deprivations of basic human need.
- Rates of absolute poverty are highest in Sub-Saharan Africa and South Asia, 65% (207 million

children) and 59% (330 million children), respectively.
- Rates are lowest in Latin America and the Caribbean and East Asia and the Pacific regions at 17% and 7%, respectively.
- Rural children face significantly higher levels of poverty than urban children, with rates for absolute poverty rising to 70% or above in both rural Sub-Saharan Africa and rural South Asia.

Summary of main results of severe deprivation of basic human need

- Over half of the world's children in developing countries (56%) – just over one billion children – are severely deprived, defined as children suffering from one or more forms of severe deprivation of basic human need.
- Two regions, South Asia and Sub-Saharan Africa, have severe deprivation rates of over 80%.
- Rural children experience much higher levels of severe deprivation than urban children. For example, more than 90% of rural children in South Asia and Sub-Saharan Africa are severely deprived of basic human needs, closely followed by rural children in the Middle East and North Africa (82%).
- Severe shelter and severe sanitation deprivation are the problems affecting the highest proportion of children in the developing world (Figure 3.1).

Figure 3.1: Percentage of children severely deprived of basic human needs

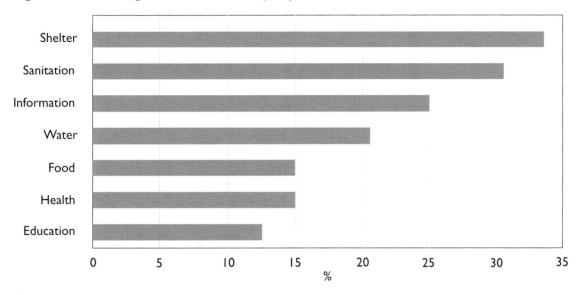

Shelter deprivation: more than a half a billion of the developing world's children (34%) have to live in dwellings with more than five people per room or which have mud flooring.

Sanitation deprivation: over half a billion children (31%) in the developing world have no toilet facilities whatsoever.

Information deprivation: almost half a billion children (25%) in the developing world lack access to radio, television, telephone or newspapers at home.

Water deprivation: nearly 376 million children (20%) in the developing world are using unsafe (open) water sources or have more than a 15-minute walk to water.

Food deprivation: over 15% of children under five years of age in the developing world are severely food deprived, over half of whom (91 million children) are in South Asia.

Health deprivation: 265 million children in the developing world (15%) have not been immunised against any diseases or have had a recent illness causing diarrhoea and have not received any medical advice or treatment.

Education deprivation: throughout the developing world, 134 million children aged between 7 and 18 (13%) are severely educationally deprived – they have never been to school.

Results by region

Sub-Saharan Africa has the highest rates of severe deprivation with respect to four of the seven indicators (Figure 3.2). More than half of this region's children are severely shelter deprived (198 million) as well as water deprived (167 million). The region also suffers from the highest rates of deprivation with respect to education (30%) and health (27%).

South Asia has the highest percentages of children experiencing sanitation, information and food deprivation, 61%, 40% and 27%, respectively. Over half of the world's severely food deprived children live in South Asia (53 million).

Children in East Asia are the least likely to be severely deprived with respect to five of the seven indicators. For example, this region has the lowest rates of severe sanitation deprivation, because China – which has a rate of less than 2% – contributes to the low regional average (5%).

The study also reveals that there may be significant differences in rates of severe deprivation among children *within* regions. For example, in Sub-Saharan Africa, only 19% of Mali children live in severely water deprived conditions, compared to 90% of Rwandan children (see Gordon et al, 2003, for other examples).

Figure 3.2: Percentage of children severely deprived, by region

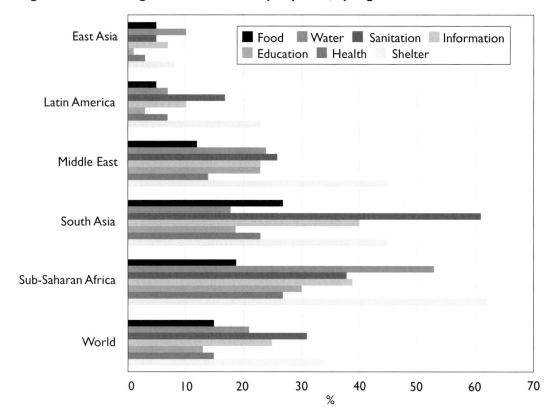

Results by rural–urban locality

Rural children are much more likely to be deprived than urban children with respect to all seven areas of deprivation of basic human need (Figure 3.3).

The greatest difference between urban and rural children is in severe sanitation deprivation (41% in rural areas compared to 9% in urban areas), but rural children are also almost three times more likely than urban children to live in very overcrowded conditions or in accommodation which has only mud flooring. The pattern of rural children's disproportionate experience of deprivation exists in all five regions.

Results by gender

Gender differences could only be meaningfully assessed where there was direct information on children (for example, in relation to food, health and education). At the global level, the study shows significant gender discrepancies in education but not in food or health deprivation (Figure 3.4). Girls are at least 60% more likely than boys to be severely educationally deprived. They suffer particularly high rates of disadvantage in the Middle East and North Africa, where they are three times more likely than boys to be without primary or secondary school education.

However, girls and boys are roughly equally disadvantaged with respect to severe food deprivation (15% and 16%, respectively) and health deprivation (15% and 14%, respectively). Boys are more likely to be severely food deprived in all regions, except South Asia where severe food deprivation is more prevalent in girls. With respect to severe health deprivation, there is a slight female disadvantage in South Asia and the Middle East and the North Africa regions. The Sub-Saharan African region has a mixed pattern of gender inequalities in health. While, at the overall level, a slightly higher proportion of boys are severely health deprived compared to girls, more than a dozen countries have a slight female disadvantage.

Figure 3.3: Percentage of rural and urban children severely deprived

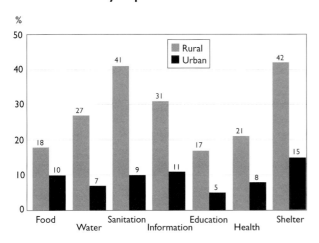

Figure 3.4: Percentage of girls and boys severely deprived

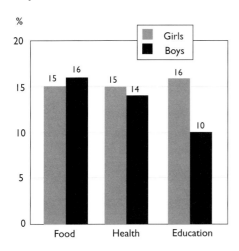

The remainder of Chapter 3 considers these findings in more detail. The first sub-section examines the extent of severe deprivation with regards to the seven basic human needs.

Extent of severe deprivation

Shelter deprivation

More than one in three (over 614 million) of all of the developing world's children experience severe shelter deprivation, defined as living in accommodation with more than five people per room or which has mud flooring (Figure 3.5 and Table 3.1).

Figure 3.5: Percentage of children suffering severe shelter deprivation

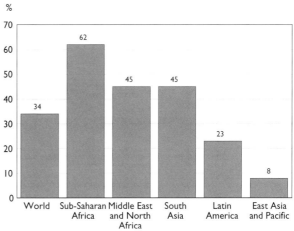

Table 3.1: Children suffering severe shelter deprivation

Region	%	Number (000s)
Latin America and Caribbean	23	43,727
South Asia	45	253,506
Middle East and North Africa	45	69,471
Sub-Saharan Africa	62	198,027
East Asia and Pacific	8	49,508
Developing world	34	614,238

The risks of experiencing shelter deprivation vary enormously between regions. Sub-Saharan Africa has a rate that is almost double the world's average, at 62%, whereas South Asia and the Middle East and North Africa have risks of 45% each. By contrast, only 8% of children living in East Asia and the Pacific are severely shelter deprived.

Rural children are significantly more likely than their urban counterparts to be living in circumstances of severe shelter deprivation (42% compared to 15%) (Figure 3.6 and Table 3.2). Whereas more than 531 million of the developing world's rural children are severely shelter deprived, *only* 83 million urban children are affected by the same conditions. However, a note of caution is required in the interpretation of these findings as the indicator of severe shelter deprivation used in this study may underestimate the dwelling-related problems

experienced by children living in urban areas, for example, homelessness.

Notwithstanding this caveat, there are important discrepancies between regions with regards to rates among rural children. Rates of severe shelter deprivation are highest for rural children in Sub-Saharan Africa (73% or 176 million children) and lowest for urban children in East Asia and the Pacific (5% or 8.5 million). Sub-Saharan Africa, as well as having the highest rates of rural children living in shelter deprivation, also has the highest proportions of urban children living in these appalling conditions (28% or 21 million children).

However, inequalities among children within regions are greatest in the Middle East and North Africa, where rural children are more than four times as likely as urban children in the same region to be severely shelter deprived (62% compared to 15%).

Figure 3.6: Percentage of rural and urban children suffering severe shelter deprivation

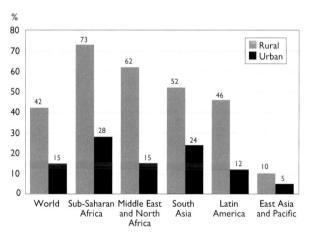

Sanitation deprivation

For the purposes of this report, severe sanitation deprivation is defined as a child having **no** access to **any** sanitation facilities of any description. Thus, children with sanitation facilities which are considered not improved (for example, public or shared latrines, open pit latrines and bucket latrines) by the Joint Monitoring Programme are *not* counted as *severely* deprived in this report, although it is acknowledged that the use of a bucket or open pit latrine is a far from appropriate or adequate method of waste disposal[3].

Table 3.2: Rural and urban children suffering severe shelter deprivation

Region	Rural children		Urban children	
		Number		Number
	%	(000s)	%	(000s)
Latin America and Caribbean	46	28,738	12	14,987
South Asia	52	223,135	24	30,142
Middle East and North Africa	62	61,288	15	8,041
Sub-Saharan Africa	73	176,336	28	21,487
East Asia and Pacific	10	41,286	5	8,511
Developing world	42	530,783	15	83,169

[3] Data concerning sanitation collected by UNICEF and the World Health Organisation (WHO) under the Joint Monitoring Programme refer to 'improved' sanitation facilities (connections to public sewers or septic systems, simple and ventilated improved pit latrines, and pour/flush latrines). 'Not improved' facilities include public or shared latrines, open pit latrines and bucket latrines.

We found that 31% of children (nearly 567 million children) in developing countries are severely sanitation deprived, lacking **any** form of sanitation facility, improved or otherwise (Figure 3.7 and Table 3.3). The lowest rate is in the East Asia and Pacific region, at 5% (30 million children) and the highest in South Asia, at 61% (344 million children). Sub-Saharan Africa also has a relatively high rate at 38% (120 million children).

Differences between urban and rural areas are considerable, confirming the findings of the 2000 *Global water supply and sanitation assessment* (GWSSA) results (WHO, UNICEF, WSSCC, 2000). At the overall level, the urban rate of severe sanitation deprivation is 9% (51 million children) (Figure 3.8 and Table 3.4). The rural rate is nearly five times higher, at 41% (516 million children). Over half a billion children in rural areas lack access to any form of sanitation facility.

Figure 3.7: Percentage of children suffering severe sanitation deprivation

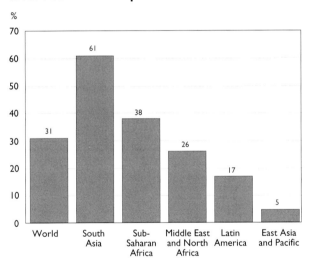

Table 3.3: Children suffering severe sanitation deprivation

Region	%	Number (000s)
Latin America and Caribbean	17	33,472
South Asia	61	343,604
Middle East and North Africa	26	39,742
Sub-Saharan Africa	38	119,833
East Asia and Pacific	5	30,188
Developing world	31	566,839

Figure 3.8: Percentage of rural and urban children suffering severe sanitation deprivation

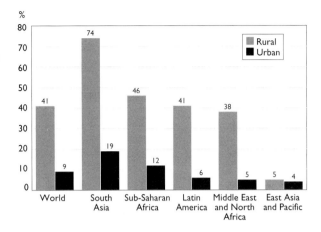

Table 3.4: Rural and urban children suffering severe sanitation deprivation

Region	Rural children %	Number (000s)	Urban children %	Number (000s)
Latin America and Caribbean	41	25,580	6	7,950
South Asia	74	319,135	19	24,292
Middle East and North Africa	38	37,250	5	2,462
Sub-Saharan Africa	46	110,902	12	8,966
East Asia and Pacific	5	23,223	4	6,948
Developing world	41	516,089	9	50,617

With regards to sanitation deprivation in urban areas, the East Asia and Pacific and Middle East and North Africa regions both have relatively low rates, at 4% (less than 7 million children) and 5% (just over 2 million children), respectively. The highest urban rate is in South Asia, at 19% (24 million children). In rural areas, the lowest rate is in the East Asia and Pacific region, at 5% (23 million children), considerably lower than all other regions – although this can be explained by the high availability of public (communal) sanitation facilities in China. Each of the other regions has rural sanitation deprivation rates above 35%, with South Asia having the highest rate of 74% (319 million children). The Sub-Saharan Africa and Latin America and Caribbean regions both have rural rates over 40%.

Information deprivation

Globally, it is estimated that 25% of all children aged three years and above are severely information deprived, representing almost 448 million children (Figure 3.9 and Table 3.5)[4]. This means that one in four children in developing countries lack access to television, radio, telephone or newspapers. Nevertheless, these global figures disguise the real magnitude of information deprivation in some regions. Analysis by region reveals that 40% of South Asian and 39% of Sub-Saharan African children suffer from severe information deprivation (226 and 124 million children, respectively). On the other hand, lower than average rates were found in the regions of Latin America and the Caribbean (10%) and East Asia and the Pacific (7%).

Severe information deprivation among children is far more extensive in rural areas than in urban areas (31% or 388 million children compared to 11% or 60 million children) (Figure 3.10 and Table 3.6). The highest rates among rural children are in South Asia at 47% (202 million children) and Sub-Saharan Africa at 45% (109 million children), while the lowest rates affect children in East Asia and the Pacific at 9% (37 million children). Among urban children, the regions with highest rates are again Sub-Saharan Africa (20%) and South Asia (19%). On the other hand, the greatest inequalities in access to information are among children living in Latin America and the Caribbean, where there are almost four rural children who are deprived for every one urban child (19% compared to *only* 5%).

Figure 3.9: Percentage of children (3 years+) suffering severe information deprivation

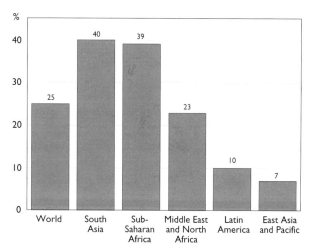

Figure 3.10: Percentage of rural and urban children (3 years+) suffering severe information deprivation

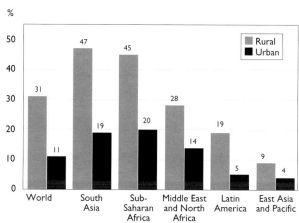

Table 3.5: Children (3 years+) suffering severe information deprivation

Region	%	Number (000s)
Latin America and Caribbean	10	18,381
South Asia	40	225,525
Middle East and North Africa	23	34,966
Sub-Saharan Africa	39	124,283
East Asia and Pacific	7	44,678
Developing world	25	447,834

[4] The authors know of no previous attempts to measure information deprivation among children.

Table 3.6: Rural and urban children (3 years+) suffering severe information deprivation

Region	Rural children Number % (000s)		Urban children Number % (000s)	
Latin America and Caribbean	19	11,748	5	6,646
South Asia	47	201,946	19	23,656
Middle East and North Africa	28	27,515	14	7,440
Sub-Saharan Africa	45	108,977	20	15,227
East Asia and Pacific	9	37,415	4	7,122
Developing world	31	387,601	11	60,090

Water deprivation

This study has estimated that 21% of children (nearly 376 million children) are severely water deprived (Figure 3.11 and Table 3.7). This means over a third of a billion children have more than a 15-minute walk to their source of water (thus limiting the quantity they use), or are using unsafe sources of water (that is, surface water). Of the five regions, the lowest rate is in the Latin America and Caribbean region, where 7% (14 million children) are severely water deprived. Sub-Saharan Africa has by far the highest rate, at 53% (167 million children). The East Asia and Pacific region has a relatively low rate of severe water deprivation, at 10% (59 million children).

There are considerable differences in children's severe water deprivation between rural and urban areas in each of the five regions (Figure 3.12 and Table 3.8). At the overall level, 7% of urban areas (nearly 41

million children) are severely water deprived. The rate in rural areas is over three times higher, at 27% (335 million children).

In urban areas, the lowest rate of severe water deprivation among children is in the Latin America and Caribbean region, at 1% (1.4 million children) and the highest urban rate is in Sub-Saharan Africa, at 19% (15 million children). The other regions all have urban rates of water deprivation below 10%.

Rates of severe water deprivation in rural areas are considerably higher. The East Asia and Pacific region has the lowest rural rate by far, at 11% (nearly 48 million children). All other regions have rural rates over 20%, with the highest in Sub-Saharan Africa at 63% (152 million children). The Middle East and North Africa region has the second highest rural rate of 34% (34 million children) although the geographic features of the region (that is, desert and

Figure 3.11: Percentage of children suffering severe water deprivation

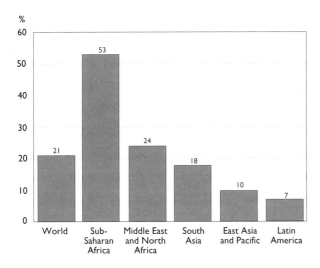

Figure 3.12: Percentage of rural and urban children suffering severe water deprivation

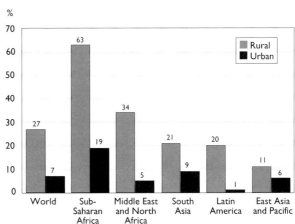

Table 3.7: Children suffering severe water deprivation

Region	%	Number (000s)
Latin America and Caribbean	7	14,318
South Asia	18	99,611
Middle East and North Africa	24	36,199
Sub-Saharan Africa	53	166,877
East Asia and Pacific	10	58,565
Developing world	21	375,569

Table 3.8: Rural and urban children suffering severe water deprivation

Region	Rural children %	Number (000s)	Urban children %	Number (000s)
Latin America and Caribbean	20	12,885	1	1,434
South Asia	21	88,649	9	11,192
Middle East and North Africa	34	33,674	5	2,626
Sub-Saharan Africa	63	152,039	19	14,685
East Asia and Pacific	11	47,737	6	10,943
Developing world	27	334,983	7	40,880

semi-desert regions) limit the availability of water. The South Asia and Latin America and Caribbean regions have similar rural rates of 21% (89 million children) and 20% (13 million children), respectively.

Food deprivation

Severe food deprivation is measured using data on severe anthropometric failure (that is, a failure to grow at normal rates to 'normal' weights and heights) in children under the age of five. Since anthropometric data are rarely collected on or available for children over five years of age, the data presented in this report only refer to children under five in developing countries.

At an overall level, it is estimated that 15% of children under five years old (representing 91 million children) in developing countries are severely food deprived (Figure 3.13 and Table 3.9). The lowest rates are in the East Asia and Pacific and Latin American and Caribbean regions, each at 5%. South

Asia has the highest overall rate at 27% (54 million children).

Differences in severe food deprivation are very pronounced between urban and rural areas. At the global level, 10% of urban children under the age of five (nearly 17 million children) and 18% of rural children under five (74 million children) are severely food deprived (Figure 3.14 and Table 3.10).

In urban areas, the lowest rate of food deprivation is in the Latin America and Caribbean region, at 3% (965,000 children) and highest in South Asia, at 19% (8 million children). In rural areas, the lowest rate is in the East Asia and Pacific region, at 4% (under 5 million children) and highest in South Asia at 29% (nearly 46 million children).

Figure 3.13: Percentage of children (<5 years) suffering severe food deprivation

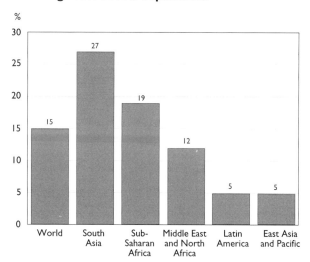

Figure 3.14: Percentage of rural and urban children (<5 years) suffering severe food deprivation

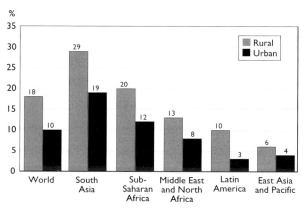

Table 3.9: Children (<5 years) suffering severe food deprivation

Region	%	Number (000s)
Latin America and Caribbean	5	2,885
South Asia	27	53,714
Middle East and North Africa	12	6,483
Sub-Saharan Africa	19	20,286
East Asia and Pacific	5	7,960
Developing world	15	91,328

Table 3.10: Rural and urban children (<5 years) suffering severe food deprivation

Region	Rural children %	Number (000s)	Urban children %	Number (000s)
Latin America and Caribbean	10	1,926	3	965
South Asia	29	45,698	19	8,067
Middle East and North Africa	13	4,955	8	1,571
Sub-Saharan Africa	20	17,102	12	2,998
East Asia and Pacific	4	4,640	6	3,352
Developing world	18	74,321	10	16,953

Gender differences in severe food deprivation appear to be relatively unimportant among children under five years of age (Figure 3.15 and Table 3.11). At the overall level, it is estimated that 16% of boys under five (48 million boys) and 15% of girls under five (44 million girls) are severely food deprived.

The Latin America and Caribbean and East Asia and Pacific regions have the lowest rates of food deprivation for boys, each at 6%. East Asia has the lowest rate for girls at 3% (just over 2 million girls). South Asia has the highest rates of food deprivation for both boys and girls, at 26% (26.5 million boys) and 28% (27 million girls). While, at the overall level, gender differences in severe food deprivation are not clear, it is apparent that slight differences do occur between regions, as Table 3.11 shows.

Health deprivation

A range of factors determines the health of children and no single indicator can sufficiently reflect the burden of disease or complete extent of morbidity. For the purposes of this report, a child was considered severely health deprived if they had not received **any** of the eight immunisations recommended by the WHO's expanded programme of immunisation (EPI) or if they had had untreated diarrhoea in the two weeks prior to the DHS survey interview.

It is estimated that, at the overall level, 15% of children in developing countries (265 million children) are severely health deprived (Figure 3.16 and Table 3.12). The lowest rate is in East Asia and the Pacific at 3% (18 million children) and the highest rates are in South Asia and Sub-Saharan Africa, with 23% (129 million children) and 27% (84 million children), respectively.

Figure 3.15: Percentage of girls and boys (<5 years) suffering severe food deprivation

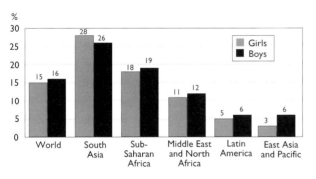

Figure 3.16: Percentage of children suffering severe health deprivation

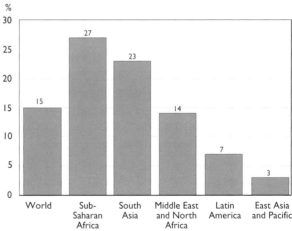

Table 3.11: Girls and boys (<5 years) suffering severe food deprivation

Region	Girls %	Girls Number (000s)	Boys %	Boys Number (000s)
Latin America and Caribbean	5	1,332	6	1,557
South Asia	28	27,257	26	26,504
Middle East and North Africa	11	3,025	12	3,494
Sub-Saharan Africa	18	9,790	19	10,501
East Asia and Pacific	3	2,323	6	5,947
Developing world	15	43,727	16	48,003

Table 3.12: Children suffering severe health deprivation

Region	%	Number (000s)
Latin America and Caribbean	7	12,770
South Asia	23	128,711
Middle East and North Africa	14	20,949
Sub-Saharan Africa	27	84,233
East Asia and Pacific	3	18,113
Developing world	15	264,776

As with the other measures of severe deprivation, there are considerable differences between urban and rural areas (Figure 3.17 and Table 3.13). Eight per cent of urban children (47 million children) and 21% of rural children (263 million children) are severely health deprived.

The lowest urban rate of child health deprivation is found in the Latin America and Caribbean region, at 4% (nearly 6 million children), although the Middle East and North Africa and East Asia and Pacific regions both have low rates, each at 6%. The highest urban rates are in Sub-Saharan Africa (13%, around 10 million children) and South Asia (14%, around 17 million children). In rural areas, the lowest rate of severe health deprivation is in the Latin America and Caribbean region, at 11% (nearly 7 million children); and the highest rate is in Sub-Saharan Africa, at 30% (73 million children).

Figure 3.18 and Table 3.14 present the data on severe health deprivation by gender. At the overall level, the rate of severe health deprivation in boys is slightly less than it is for girls, 14% (133 million boys) compared to 15% (132 million girls). At the regional level, the lowest rate of severe health deprivation for boys is in East Asia and the Pacific, at 3% (10 million boys). The highest rate for boys is in Sub-Saharan Africa, at 27% (43 million boys). The East Asia and Pacific region also has the lowest rate for girls, at 3% (under 9 million girls) and Sub-Saharan Africa again has the highest rate, at 26% (41 million girls).

It should be noted that diseases such as pneumonia, malaria and tuberculosis, which account for a large proportion of child deaths and ill-health in the developing world, are not measured by these data. It is likely that the burden of ill-health is actually far greater than is implied by the measures of severe health deprivation used in this report. What is certain

Figure 3.17: Percentage of rural and urban children suffering severe health deprivation

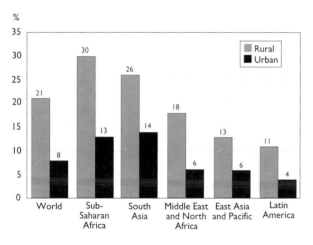

Figure 3.18: Percentage of girls and boys suffering severe health deprivation

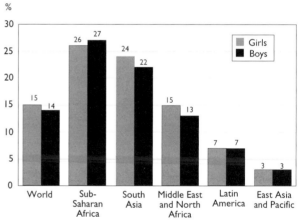

Table 3.13: Rural and urban children suffering severe health deprivation

Region	Rural children %	Rural children Number (000s)	Urban children %	Urban children Number (000s)
Latin America and Caribbean	11	6,821	4	5,734
South Asia	26	110,703	14	17,169
Middle East and North Africa	18	17,482	6	3,392
Sub-Saharan Africa	30	72,652	13	9,971
East Asia and Pacific	13	55,478	6	10,769
Developing world	21	263,136	8	47,035

Table 3.14: Girls and boys suffering severe health deprivation

Region	Girls %	Girls Number (000s)	Boys %	Boys Number (000s)
Latin America and Caribbean	7	6,497	7	6,366
South Asia	24	65,245	22	63,555
Middle East and North Africa	15	11,118	13	9,864
Sub-Saharan Africa	26	40,661	27	43,436
East Asia and Pacific	3	8,633	3	10,124
Developing world	15	132,144	14	133,345

is that the decline of public health systems and services means that appropriate care is rarely available, affordable or provided, and so increasing numbers of children will continue to suffer and die from a range of causes, a large number of which (such as diarrhoea and the EPI six targeted diseases) are preventable.

Education deprivation

Throughout the developing world, 13% of all children (134 million) aged between 7 and 18 are severely educationally deprived, defined as lacking any primary or secondary school education, that is, never having gone to school (Figure 3.19 and Table 3.15). Sub-Saharan Africa has an above-average rate of 30% (50 million children), as do the Middle East and North African (23% or 19 million children) and South Asian (19% or 57 million children) regions, whereas Latin America and the Caribbean and East Asia have relatively low rates, at 3% and 1%, respectively.

There are significant urban–rural differences in lack of access to education. Seventeen per cent of all rural children aged between 7 and 18 experience severe education deprivation, compared to *only* 5% of all urban children (Figure 3.20 and Table 3.16). Rates of severe educational deprivation are higher among rural children in every single region of the developing world. The Middle East and North Africa and Sub-Saharan Africa regions have well above-average rates of severe education deprivation among rural children, at 33% and 35%, respectively.

With regards to urban children, higher than average prevalence rates of educational deprivation exist in the Sub-Saharan Africa and South Asia regions (13% and 10%, respectively). Some regions exhibit large inequalities between urban and rural children. For example, rural children in the Middle East and North

Figure 3.19: Percentage of children (aged 7-18) suffering severe educational deprivation

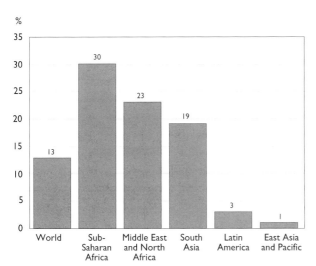

Figure 3.20: Percentage of rural and urban children (aged 7-18) suffering severe educational deprivation

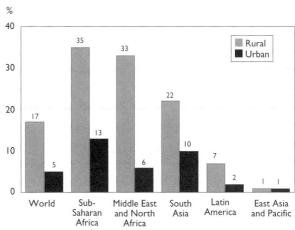

Table 3.15: Children (aged 7-18) suffering severe educational deprivation

Region	%	Number (000s)
Latin America and Caribbean	3	4,028
South Asia	19	57,134
Middle East and North Africa	23	18,608
Sub-Saharan Africa	30	50,274
East Asia and Pacific	1	4,139
Developing world	13	134,183

Table 3.16: Rural and urban (aged 7-18) children suffering severe educational deprivation

Region	Rural children %	Number (000s)	Urban children %	Number (000s)
Latin America and Caribbean	7	2,428	2	1,541
South Asia	22	50,055	10	6,892
Middle East and North Africa	33	16,877	6	1,768
Sub-Saharan Africa	35	44,700	13	5,556
East Asia and Pacific	1	3,542	1	623
Developing world	17	117,602	5	16,380

Africa are at least five times more likely than their urban counterparts to be severely educationally deprived (33% compared to *only* 6%).

Girls are much more likely than boys to be at risk of being educationally deprived. Globally, they are over one-and-a-half times more likely than boys to suffer severe educational deprivation (16% compared to 10%) (Figure 3.21 and Table 3.17). There are also many more educationally deprived girls than boys throughout the world. It is estimated that 80 million girls have received neither a primary nor secondary school education, compared to 54 million boys.

This study also reveals significant gender discrepancies in access to education both between regions and within them. The regions of the Middle East and North Africa and Sub-Saharan Africa have above-average deprivation rates among girls, at 34% and 32%, respectively. However, the greatest gender

inequalities exist in the Middle East and North Africa region where educationally deprived girls outnumber boys by almost three to one. The East Asia and the Pacific region has the greatest gender equality with respect to access to education, whereas Latin America and the Caribbean reveals a very small gender bias *against* boys rather than girls.

Distribution of severe deprivation

This next section looks at the distribution of severe deprivation among the regions of the developing world. For the purposes of this study, severe deprivation has been defined as children experiencing one or more severe deprivations of basic human need. Figure 3.22 and Table 3.18 show the number and proportion of children in the five UNICEF regions suffering one or more severe deprivations.

Figure 3.21: Percentage of girls and boys (aged 7-18) suffering severe educational deprivation

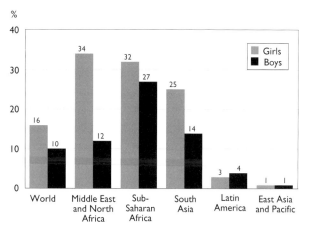

Figure 3.22: Percentage of children suffering severe deprivation

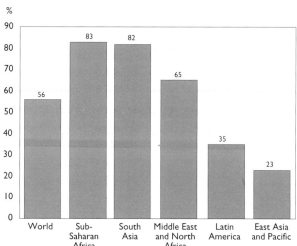

Table 3.17: Girls and boys (aged 7-18) suffering severe educational deprivation

Region	Girls %	Girls Number (000s)	Boys %	Boys Number (000s)
Latin America and Caribbean	3	1,822	4	2,148
South Asia	25	35,983	14	21,015
Middle East and North Africa	34	13,491	12	5,100
Sub-Saharan Africa	32	27,056	27	23,293
East Asia and Pacific	1	1,946	1	2,123
Developing world	16	80,299	10	53,679

Table 3.18: Children suffering severe deprivation

Region	%	Number (000s)
Latin America and Caribbean	35	68,493
South Asia	82	459,444
Middle East and North Africa	65	99,354
Sub-Saharan Africa	83	264,460
East Asia and Pacific	23	137,054
Developing world	56	1,028,804

At the global level, 56% of children in the developing world (more than 1 billion children) are severely deprived of basic human needs. The lowest rate is in the East Asia and Pacific region (23%), while rates are highest in South Asia (82%) and Sub-Saharan Africa (83%). All but two of the regions have severe deprivation rates above 50%.

Approximately a third of children (over 175 million) in urban areas and two thirds of children (853 million) in rural areas are severely deprived of basic human needs (Figure 3.23 and Table 3.19).

The East Asia and Pacific region has the lowest rates for both urban and rural areas, at 17% and 25% respectively, while Sub-Saharan Africa has the highest rates for both urban and rural areas, at 53% and 93%. South Asia has the largest numbers of children living in severe deprivation in both urban and rural areas (61 million children and 398 million children, respectively).

Distribution of absolute poverty

The final section of this chapter compares the extent of absolute poverty among the different regions in the developing world. For the purposes of this report, absolute poverty is defined as multiple severe deprivation of basic human need – that is, children suffering from two or more different severe deprivations.

More than one third (37%) of the developing world's children (over 674 million children) are living in absolute poverty. The lowest rate is found in the East Asia and Pacific region, at 7% (43 million children) and the highest rate is in Sub-Saharan Africa, at 65% (nearly 207 million children). South Asia also has a high rate of absolute poverty, with 59% (330 million children) of children suffering two or more forms of severe deprivation.

Figure 3.23: Percentage of rural and urban children suffering severe deprivation

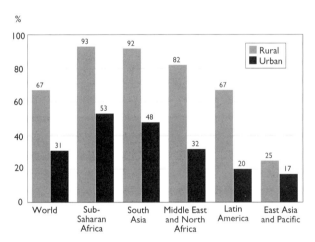

Table 3.19: Rural and urban children suffering severe deprivation

Region	Rural children %	Rural children Number (000s)	Urban children %	Urban children Number (000s)
Latin America and Caribbean	67	42,570	20	25,934
South Asia	92	398,270	48	61,174
Middle East and North Africa	82	81,651	32	17,669
Sub-Saharan Africa	93	223,969	53	40,578
East Asia and Pacific	25	106,656	17	30,050
Developing world	67	853,115	31	175,405

Figure 3.24: Percentage of children in absolute poverty

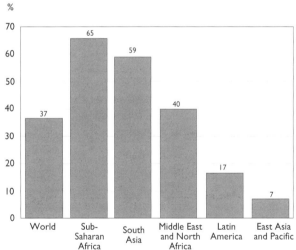

Table 3.20: Children suffering from absolute poverty

Region	%	Number (000s)
Latin America and Caribbean	17	33,085
South Asia	59	329,613
Middle East and North Africa	40	61,153
Sub-Saharan Africa	65	206,927
East Asia and Pacific	7	43,471
Developing world	37	674,249

Most children in absolute poverty live in rural areas, although rates in the urban areas of some regions are also high (Figure 3.25 and Table 3.21). The urban rate of absolute poverty is 12% (65 million children), while the rural rate is much higher at 48% (610 million children).

Figure 3.25: Percentage of rural and urban children in absolute poverty

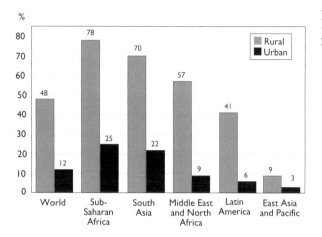

Table 3.21: Rural and urban children in absolute poverty

Region	Rural children		Urban children	
	%	**Number (000s)**	**%**	**Number (000s)**
Latin America and Caribbean	41	25,769	6	7,168
South Asia	70	301,838	22	28,234
Middle East and North Africa	57	56,222	9	4,978
Sub-Saharan Africa	78	188,124	25	19,014
East Asia and Pacific	9	38,276	3	5,385
Developing world	48	610,229	12	64,778

The lowest urban and rural rates of absolute poverty are found in the East Asia and Pacific region, at 3% (just over 5 million children) and 9% (38 million children), respectively. The highest urban rates of absolute poverty are in Sub-Saharan Africa and South Asia; with the former's urban absolute poverty rate at 25% (19 million children) compared to South Asia's 22% (28 million children). Absolute poverty rates in rural areas are above 50% in all regions (except Latin America and the Caribbean and East Asia and Pacific), with rates in both South Asia and Sub-Saharan Africa at 70% or more.

Conclusions and policy implications

Over one billion children – **more than half** the children in developing countries – suffer from severe deprivation of basic human need and **over one third** (674 million) suffer from absolute poverty (two or more severe deprivations).

- Over one third of children have to live in dwellings with more than five people per room or which have a mud flooring.
- Over half a billion children (31%) have no toilet facilities whatsoever.
- Almost half a billion children (25%) lack access to radio, television, telephone or newspapers at home.
- Over 20% of children (nearly 376 million) have more than a 15-minute walk to water or are using unsafe (open) water sources.
- Over 15% of children under-five years in the developing world are severely food deprived, over half of whom (91 million children) are in South Asia.
- 265 million children (15%) have not been immunised against any diseases or have had a recent illness involving diarrhoea and have not received any medical advice or treatment.
- 134 million children aged between 7 and 18 (13%) are severely educationally deprived in terms of lacking any school education whatsoever.
- There are differences both *between* and *within* regions that are masked by the overall average rates. For example, Sub-Saharan Africa has the highest rates of severe deprivation with respect to four of the seven indicators – severe shelter, water, educational and health deprivation. However, within the region, only 19% of Mali children live in severely water deprived conditions, compared to 90% of Rwandan children.
- Rural children are much more likely to be deprived than urban children in all seven areas of deprivation of basic human need and in all regions. This is particularly the case with respect to severe sanitation deprivation.
- At the global level, there are significant gender differences with girls more likely to be severely educationally deprived, particularly in the Middle East and North Africa, where they are three times more likely than boys to be without primary or secondary school education.

These findings are shocking given that severe deprivations of basic human need are those circumstances that are highly likely to have serious adverse consequences for the health, well-being and development of children. Severe deprivations harm children in both the short term and the long term. Many of the absolutely poor children surveyed in this research will have died or had their health profoundly damaged by the time this report is published, as a direct consequence of their appalling living conditions. Many others will have had their development so severely impaired that they may be unable to escape from a lifetime of grinding poverty.

The definitions used in this study to identify severe deprivation of children's basic human needs represent much worse living conditions than are usually reported by UN agencies. This research has measured absolute poverty using such severe criteria that any reasonable person would consider that these living conditions were unacceptable and damaging. No government or parent wants children to have to live like this. This final chapter looks at what lessons can be learnt from this research and what could be done to help eradicate absolute child poverty during the 21st century.

The causes of absolute poverty

Absolute poverty has been measured within the internationally agreed framework of children's rights, using a definition of absolute poverty that has been agreed to by 117 governments as: "a condition characterised by severe deprivation of basic human needs, including food, safe drinking water, sanitation facilities, health, shelter, education and information. It depends not only on income but also on access to social services".

This research has shown that the severe deprivations that affect the greatest number of children are shelter, sanitation, information and water deprivation. Fewer children suffer from severe deprivation of food, health and education. This, in part, demonstrates the partial success of international agencies and donors that have focused on improving children's access to health and education services and preventing malnutrition.

However, lessons need to be drawn from the experiences of industrialised countries in combating poverty and improving children's health. During the 19th and first half of the 20th centuries, the most important improvements in standard of living and life expectancy of children in industrialised countries were as a result of significant public investment in housing, sewerage and water systems. Safe water, housing and sanitation facilities are prerequisites for good health and education. If children are made chronically sick as a result of unsafe water supplies or inadequate sanitation or overcrowded housing conditions, then they cannot go to school even if free high quality education is available. Similarly, good health facilities can help alleviate the symptoms of chronic sickness but they cannot tackle the underlying causes. Food aid will not be effective in reducing malnutrition if children suffer from chronic diarrhoea as a result of a lack of sanitation facilities and/or unsafe water.

The evidence presented in this report points to the conclusion that UN and other international agencies, governments and donors may need to give a higher priority to tackling the problems of severe shelter,

sanitation and water deprivation than is presently the case.

There has been some recent debate within the international community about the need to tackle the problems of housing, water and sanitation deprivation. However, much of this debate has focused on facilitating the private sector to provide additional investment and infrastructure in urban areas. This research shows that far more children in rural areas suffer from severe deprivation than their urban peers[5]. Since the prime motivation of the private sector is the need to optimise profits, it is extremely unlikely that it will be able to provide water and sewerage infrastructure to all poor rural areas, as this would not be profitable. The only way to provide all absolutely poor rural children with adequate housing, sanitation and water facilities is by public investment to pay for these infrastructure facilities. International agencies could be more active in campaigning for greater shelter, sanitation and water infrastructure investment in rural areas of the developing world. Improvements to this rural infrastructure would be the most effective method of reducing absolute child poverty.

Sanitation

Children are particularly affected by poor sanitation, since it is directly linked to the most serious of childhood illnesses – diarrhoea and malnutrition. Sanitation facilities provided for communities may often be unsuitable for children. If facilities are constructed for adults, they may be too large for young children and present obvious dangers (such as falling in); facilities lacking adequate lighting may intimidate young children wanting to use them at night; children wanting to use public facilities may be made to wait while adults use them first, and so on. The needs of adolescent girls and young women for sanitation and privacy also need to be a priority.

---

[5] Approximately 530 million rural children suffer from severe shelter deprivation compared with 85 million urban children; 515 million rural children suffer from severe sanitation deprivation compared with 50 million urban children; 335 million rural children suffer from severe water deprivation compared with 40 million urban children – see Chapter 3 for details.

Sanitation facilities require effective drainage systems that carry sewage away from communities. Children use fields and open spaces to play, areas that are commonly used for defecation in the absence of public or private facilities. Organisations like UNICEF and the World Bank are already committed to improving children's access to sanitation and should support organisations that try to establish and maintain public sanitation facilities. Such organisations have started to provide child-friendly facilities, which children can use in safety, without fear or intimidation[6]. The provision of sanitation facilities in schools is also important and should be supported.

There has been some reluctance in the past to highlight the need to improve sanitation facilities as many people do not like to talk about human excreta disposal and donors have gained greater positive publicity for helping improve children's health and education facilities than for funding latrines. Organisations like UNICEF could play a lead role in both raising funds and highlighting the crucial importance of eradicating severe sanitation deprivation as a method of helping eradicate absolute child poverty. Toilet facilities are clearly a priority for children.

Water

Severe water deprivation is an issue of both quality and quantity. Improving water quality is clearly important for the health of children. Children should not have to use unsafe (or unimproved) sources of water, such as lakes, ponds or streams, as these may become contaminated and dangerous. Communities need to have access to safe water (piped water, stand-pumps, covered wells and so on),

---

[6] One non-governmental organisation running such schemes is Gramalaya. Based in Tamil Nadu in India, the scheme came about after consultation with the local community. Facilities are constructed adjacent to community toilets. Water with soap is provided for hand washing after defecation. A caretaker from the community toilet teaches hand washing and its importance to the children and observes children's hygiene behaviours. Facilities are provided free to children (http://gramalaya.org/childtoilets.html).

through services that they can afford, run and maintain themselves. Such facilities will need to be located and provided near to where people live, to cut journey times for collection. Distance to the water source is of special significance to children since they often help collect and carry the water. Carrying water over long distances can result in injuries, especially to necks and backs, and the time spent collecting water can impact on school attendance.

The distance children need to go in order to get to their water supply is arguably of greater importance than water quality (Esrey, 1996). Water quantity is directly linked to distance to water supply, with less water used the further away the water source. The measure of severe water deprivation used in this report takes into account the issue of distance to water source – something the Joint Monitoring Programme (JMP) of UNICEF and WHO does not, that is, it focuses on water quality issues only. It is important that international organisations, governments and donors take steps to help increase both the quality and quantity of water available to poor children if absolute poverty is to be eradicated.

Shelter

Overcrowded dwellings facilitate the transmission of disease (for example, respiratory infections, measles). They can also result in increased stress and mental health problems for both adults and children and lead to accidents and injuries. Poor quality shelter, constructed from inferior materials, does not protect against the elements. Successive UN conferences and conventions have sought to address the issue of poor housing and shelter deprivation in both developed and developing countries but progress on meeting children's basic shelter needs has been slow. Considerable international attention has focused on improving the housing conditions of urban slums, shanty towns and favelas. However, this research shows that severe shelter deprivation blights the lives of 42% of rural children in developing countries, compared with 15% of children in urban areas. Improving the housing conditions of families with children in rural areas needs to be given greater priority.

Food

This research used severe anthropometric failure, that is, children more than −3 standard deviations below the international reference population median, as a measure of severe food deprivation. However, data on children's height and weights are only usually collected for children up to five years old. There is good scientific evidence that older children (particularly during puberty) may also be at risk of suffering from malnutrition. Anthropometric data on older children need to be collected, so that more accurate estimates of child malnutrition in the developing world can be made.

A technical innovation of this research has been the development and use of a Composite Index of Anthropometric Failure (CIAF), based on the work of Peter Svedberg (2000). It provides a more comprehensive indicator of malnutrition than existing measures, and thus may be more appropriate for use in target setting and resource allocation. UNICEF may want to consider development of this indicator and its potential use to monitor the international commitments to reduce child malnutrition by half by 2015. A number of countries, such as Thailand and Costa Rica, have managed to eradicate severe malnutrition and reduce mild-moderate malnutrition relatively quickly. Their success was based on clear political commitment to reducing malnutrition, the provision of food subsidies, the targeting of food supplements to children and mothers, health and nutrition education and regular growth monitoring and surveillance (ACC/SCN, 2002).

Child and family benefit

Another lesson that can be drawn from the experiences of industrialised countries in reducing child poverty is that, after public infrastructure investment, the most effective anti-poverty policy for children is the establishment of a child or family social security benefit.

It has been argued elsewhere (Townsend and Gordon, 2002) that an international children's investment fund should be established under the auspices of the UN. Half its annual resources should be devoted to countries with extensive child poverty, where schemes of child benefit in cash or kind exist or where such schemes can be introduced. All countries with large numbers of children who are below an internationally recognised poverty line and also with comparatively low GDP should be entitled to participate. Such participation would require dependable information that the benefits are reaching children for whom they are intended. The remaining annual resources of the fund would be made available to countries for investment in housing, sanitation and water infrastructure, education, health and other schemes of direct benefit to children.

Programmes to gradually increase public expenditure so that categories of the extreme poor start to benefit offer a realistic, affordable and successful method for poverty alleviation. For example, in Brazil, the Zero Hunger Programme intends to provide regular and sufficient supplies of quality food to all Brazilians in conjunction with accelerated social security reform. The first includes food banks, popular restaurants, food cards, distribution of emergency food baskets, strengthening of family agriculture and a variety of other measures to fight malnutrition. The social security reform programme includes social assistance for low-income 15- to 17-year-olds, assistance for 7- to 14-year-olds who are enabled to go to school and avoid the exacting toll of the worst conditions of child labour, minimum income and food scholarships for pregnant and nursing mothers with incomes less than half the minimum wage or who are HIV positive, benefits for elderly disabled people with special needs and a range of other transfer programmes for the elderly, widowed, sick and industrially injured and unemployed that are being enlarged year by year (Suplicy, 2003: forthcoming).

The social security systems of developing countries present a diverse picture. Partial systems were introduced by colonial authorities in most of Asia, Africa and the Caribbean. They were extended in the first instance to civil servants and employees of large enterprises. There were benefits for relatively small groups that included healthcare, maternity leave, disability allowances and pensions (Midgeley, 1984; Ahmad et al, 1991). In India, there are differences among major states as well as a range of schemes for smallish categories of population (Ghai, 2001; Prabhu, 2001). In Latin America, some countries introduced schemes before the 1939-45 war and others followed suit after. Benefits tended to be limited in range and coverage. There were different systems for particular occupations and categories of workers and a multiplicity of institutions. Between 20 and 60% of the workforce were covered, compared with between 5 and 10% for most of Sub-Saharan Africa and 10 to 30% for most of Asia. "The greatest challenge facing the developing countries is to extend the benefits of social security to the excluded majority to enable them to cope with indigence and social contingencies" (Huber, 1996).

These recommendations are the key to a far better future for hundreds of millions of children. But how might social security systems now evolve to provide universal beneficial effects of more substantial redistribution? Human rights now play a central part in discussions of international social policy. This applies to civil and political rights, less so to social and economic rights. Articles 22 and 25 in the Declaration of Human Rights – dealing with the rights to an 'adequate' standard of living and social security – have been often overlooked in General Assembly and other reports from the UN. The fundamental right to social security is also spelt out in Article 26 of the Convention on the Rights of the Child and the related rights to an adequate standard of living in Article 27.

UNICEF and other international organisations (such as the International Labour Organization [ILO]) should campaign for a legal right to child benefit under Articles 25 and 27 of the Convention on the Rights of the Child.

The needs of children in the 21st century

The needs of children in the 21st century are different from those of children in the 19th and 20th centuries and new policies will be required to meet these needs. For example, in the 21st century, severe information deprivation is an important constraint on the development of both individual children and societies as a whole – many consider that 'knowledge is power'. This study provides the first estimates of the extent of severe information deprivation among children. A quarter of children in the developing world are severely information deprived, with

approximately 390 million living in rural areas and 60 million living in urban areas.

Reducing information deprivation will require action at a number of different levels, including getting children into school and increasing literacy rates for both children and adults. Without these basic essentials, the impact and provision of newspapers and other media (such as computers and the Internet) will be limited.

The most cost-effective intervention is through improvements to radio access. Radio is one of the main channels of information in developing countries. They are a cheap, effective means through which communities can be informed about the importance of education and health initiatives (for example, immunisation for young children, the benefits of hand washing, effective and cheap ways to treat diarrhoea, availability of food supplements for malnourished children, and so on). All countries have the means to make radio broadcasts. Governments could improve public information services and regularly broadcast programmes that inform communities about simple but effective changes they can make to their lives – for example, making simple water filters using locally available materials, constructing basic sanitation facilities at low cost, and so on. The development of cheap clockwork radios has meant the technology can be made widely available, at an affordable price.

There are many examples of community radio networks that have an important role in the provision of public information (for example, the Developing Countries Farm Radio Network[7], the World

---

[7] Developing Countries Farm Radio Network is a Canadian-based, not-for-profit organisation working in partnership with approximately 500 radio broadcasters in over 70 countries to fight poverty and food insecurity. It supports broadcasters in meeting the needs of local small-scale farmers and their families in rural communities and helps broadcasters build the skills to develop content that responds to local needs (www.farmradio.org).

Community Radio Movement[8], Community Radios Worldwide[9]). Community organisations have campaigned for the installation of small, local transmitters that can provide information to local communities. They have also argued for the granting of broadcast licences to women's groups, local colleges and universities, cooperatives, and so on. However, commercialisation of the airwaves and the imposition of license fees have begun to affect community radio stations, as they are pushed aside by commercial broadcasters.

Governments might consider allocating resources to the development of community media funds that would provide information over the airwaves on important issues such as health and education. UN organisations like the Food and Agriculture Organisation and the United Nations Educational, Scientific and Cultural Organization (UNESCO) have been committed to community media and radio networks for a number of years and support initiatives providing information to rural areas (Hughes, 2001; Ilboudo, 2001). As one UNESCO report stated:

> Community radio is low-cost, easy to operate, reaches all segments of the community through local languages and can offer information, education, entertainment, as well as a platform for debate and cultural expression. As a grass-roots channel of communication, it maximises the potential for development to be drawn from sharing the information, knowledge and skills already existing within the community. It can therefore act as a catalyst for community and individual empowerment. (Hughes, 2001)

UN agencies could help inform both governments and the public on the importance of information access for children and thereby raise the profile of this issue. They might also assist in the setting up of local radio networks, and help train communities in accessing and using information effectively.

---

8   AMARC is an international NGO serving the community radio movement, with almost 3,000 members and associates in 106 countries. Its goal is to support and contribute to the development of community and participatory radio along the principles of solidarity and international cooperation (www.amarc.org/amarc/ang/).

9   www.radiorobinhood.fi/communityradios/articles

The poverty of girls

This study found that gender differences at the global level were greatest for severe education deprivation, with girls 60% more likely to be deprived. Significant regional and country disparities were revealed in the study, with girls in the Middle East and North Africa region three times more likely to be severely education deprived.

The reasons why children (and particularly girls) do not go to school vary and policies need to be targeted at the causes of non-attendance if they are to be effective. For example, children may not attend school because there is no school close enough or because it is too expensive or because the quality of the education is poor or because there is discrimination against girls going to school.

Abolishing primary school fees may encourage and enable poor parents to send their children – and particularly their daughters – to school. In some countries, there needs to be a concurrent effort made to change social attitudes about the value of education for girls. This applies to all levels of society including parents, politicians and schoolteachers. There are other practical interventions that can be pursued including the provision of incentives such as bursaries, free school meals and books, improved sanitation facilities and security. As part of the global Education For All campaign, UNESCO recently recommended a number of activities that governments should undertake to meet the goals of eliminating gender disparities in education by 2005 and achieving gender equality by 2015. These included:

- setting concrete targets and funding them adequately;
- educating mothers – the most crucial measure for the sustained education of girls;
- supporting gender-responsive schools and allowing pregnant girls and teenage mothers to continue their education;
- making educational content relevant to local cultural and economic contexts so that parents see that educating girls improves their quality of life;
- providing gender-sensitive curricula and textbooks;
- training more female teachers and make teacher training gender responsive;

- eliminating child labour. According to a recent ILO report, 352 million children between the ages of 5 and 17 are engaged in economic activities, of which 168 million are girls;
- including HIV/AIDS prevention in the curriculum;
- education is a powerful 'social vaccine' against the HIV/AIDS pandemic. Learning methods should address the fact that girls are heading households, caring for siblings and being forced to generate income;
- building schools closer to girls' homes to increase access, particularly for rural children;
- making schools safe for girls and equipping them with separate toilets.

Regional and country-specific anti-poverty policies

This research has found that the major causes of absolute child poverty vary both between and within regions of the developing world. For the world as a whole, shelter combined with sanitation deprivation affects the greatest number of children. Whereas shelter combined with water deprivation is the biggest problem in Sub-Saharan Africa, in South Asia, almost 36% of households with children suffer from shelter and information deprivation. By contrast, in the Middle East and North African region, shelter combined with education deprivation affects the greatest number of poor children. It is clear that, in order to eradicate absolute poverty among children, policies will need to be targeted at the various problems they face. A single set of anti-poverty policies for the planet is not the most effective or efficient way to eradicate child poverty. Aid donors and international agencies need to be aware – and make the public aware – of the need for tailored anti-poverty strategies which deal with the 'real' problems faced by children in different countries. Investment in eradicating severe educational deprivation may be a very effective means of reducing absolute child poverty in some countries in North Africa and the Middle East but it would be much less effective in Latin America or South Asia where ending other severe child deprivations should be prioritised.

This report has shown – for the first time – the true extent of the scale and nature of absolute child poverty in the developing world. It has used internationally agreed definitions of poverty and applied a sound, scientific methodology that shows that over half a billion children in the developing world live in absolute poverty. However, due to the severity of the measures used, this is likely to be an underestimate. Research and reports from a number of international organisations (WHO, 2001; Vandemoortele, 2002; UNDP, 2003) suggest that the optimism shown at the end of the last millennium was either premature or misplaced. It is sadly the case that there is growing recognition of the fact that most of the Millennium Development Goals will not be met in time on current trends. Issues such as international debt, unequal trade and economic relations, declining donor commitment to international aid, and increasing political and economic instability continue to work together to undermine the efforts of governments, international and non-governmental organisations, communities and individuals. As things stand today (and as this report shows), the campaign to eradicate child poverty still has a long way to go.

References

ACC/SCN (2002) *Ending malnutrition by 2020: An agenda for change in the millennium*, Commission on the Nutrition Challenges of the 21st Century, ACC/SCN: Geneva.

Ahmad, E., Dreze, J., Hills, J. and Sen, A. (1991) *Social security in developing countries*, Oxford: Clarendon Press.

Atkinson, A.B. (1990) *Comparing poverty rates internationally: Lessons from recent studies in OECD countries*, Welfare State Programme/53, London: London School of Economics and Political Science.

Bauer, R.A. (1966) *Social indicators*, Cambridge, MA: MIT Press.

Boltvinik, J. (1999) *Poverty measurement methods: An overview*, UNDP Social Development and Poverty Elimination Division Poverty Reduction Series, available from www.undp.org/poverty/publications/pov_red/Poverty_Measurement_Methods.pdf

Brown, M. and Madge, N. (1982) *Despite the welfare state: A report on the SSRC/DHSS programme of research into transmitted deprivation*, SSRC/DHSS Studies in Deprivation and Disadvantage, London: Heinemann Educational Books.

Comparative Research Programme on Poverty (2001) *A critical review of the World Bank Report: World Development Report 2000/2001. Attacking poverty*, Bergen, Norway: CROP, available at www.crop.org/publications/files/report/Comments_to_WDR2001_2002_ny.pdf

Esrey, S.A. (1996) 'No half measures – sustaining health from water and sanitation systems', *Waterlines*, vol 14, no 3, pp 24-7.

Ghai, D. (2001) 'Social security for all', *Technical Commissions*, Leo Wildmann Symposium, Stockholm, September, International Social Security Association, Geneva.

Goodman, A. and Webb, S. (1995) *The distribution of UK household expenditure, 1979-92*, IFS Commentary No 49, London: Institute for Fiscal Studies.

Gordon, D. (2002) 'The international measurement of poverty and anti-poverty policies', in P. Townsend and D. Gordon (eds) *World poverty: New policies to defeat an old enemy*, Bristol: The Policy Press, pp 53-80.

Gordon, D. and Spicker, P. (eds) (1998) *The international glossary on poverty*, London: Zed Books.

Gordon, D., Nandy, S., Pantazis, C. and Townsend, P. (with Minujin, A., Vandemoortele, J. and Namazie, C.) (2001) *Child rights and child poverty in developing countries*, Bristol: University of Bristol.

Gordon, D., Nandy, S., Pantazis, C., Pemberton, S. and Townsend, P. (2003) *The distribution of child poverty in the developing world*, Bristol: University of Bristol.

Huber, E. (1996) 'Options for social policy in Latin America: neo-liberal versus democratic models', in G. Esping-Andersen (ed) *Welfare states in transition*, Geneva and London: UNRISD and Sage Publications.

Hughes, S. (2001) *Community multimedia centres: Integrating modern and traditional information and communication technologies for community development – A programme addressing the digital divide in some of the poorest communities of the developing world*, Paris: UNESCO, available at www.fao.org/docrep/003/x6721e/x6721e17.htm

Ilboudo, J.P. (2001) *FAO's experience in the area of rural radio, including information and communication technologies servicing rural radio: New contents, new partnerships*, Rome: FAO, available at www.fao.org/docrep/003/x6721e/x6721e38.htm#P5_1

Langmore, J. (2000) 'Reducing poverty: the implications of the 1995 Copenhagen Agreement for research on poverty', in D. Gordon and P. Townsend (eds) *Breadline Europe: The measurement of poverty*, Bristol: The Policy Press, pp 35-47.

Mehrotra, S., Vandemoortele, J. and Delamonica, E. (2000) *Basic services for all? Public spending and the social dimensions of poverty*, Florence, Italy: UNICEF Innocenti Research Centre, available at www.unicef-icdc.org/publications/pdf/basice.pdf

Midgeley, J. (1984) *Social security, inequality and the third world*, New York, NY: Wiley.

Milanovic, B. (2002) 'True world income distribution, 1988 and 1993: first calculations based on household surveys alone', *The Economic Journal*, vol 112, pp 51-92.

Øyen, E., Miller, S.M. and Samad, S.A. (1996) *Poverty: A global review. Handbook on international poverty research*, Scandinavian University Press.

Prabhu, K.S. (2001) *Socio-economic security in the context of pervasive poverty: A case study of India*, SES Papers, Geneva: ILO.

Reddy, S.G. and Pogge, T.W. (2002) *How not to count the poor*, Columbia University, available at www.socialanalysis.org

Rowntree, B.S. (1901) *Poverty: A study of town life*, London: Macmillan. Recently re-published in 2000 by The Policy Press (see www.bris.ac.uk/Publications/TPP/pages/at036.htm).

Sachs, J.D., Mellinger, A.D. and Gallup, J.L. (2001) 'The geography of poverty and wealth', *Scientific American*, March, vol 284, no 3, pp 70-5, details available at www.cid.harvard.edu/cidinthenews/articles/Sciam_0301.html

Sen, A. (1981) *Poverty and famines: An essay on entitlement and deprivation*, Oxford: Clarendon Press.

Suplicy, E.M. (2003: forthcoming) *President Lula's Zero Hunger Programme and the trend toward a citizen's basic income in Brazil*, London: London School of Economics and Political Science.

Svedberg, P. (2000) *Poverty and undernutrition: Theory, measurement and policy*, New Delhi: Oxford University Press.

Townsend, P. (1979) *Poverty in the United Kingdom*, London: Allen Lane and Penguin Books.

Townsend, P. (1987) 'Deprivation', *Journal of Social Policy*, vol 16, no 2, pp 125-46.

Townsend, P. and Gordon, D. (eds) (2002) *World poverty: New policies to defeat an old enemy*, Bristol: The Policy Press.

UN (United Nations) (1995) *The Copenhagen Declaration and Programme of Action: World Summit for Social Development 6-12 March 1995*, New York, NY: UNDP.

UN General Assembly (2002) *We the children: End-decade review of the follow-up to the World Summit for Children*, Report of the Secretary-General, New York, NY: UN.

UNDP (United Nations Development Programme) (2003) *Human Development Report 2003*, New York, NY: UNDP.

UNICEF (United Nations Children's Fund) (2000) *Poverty reduction begins with children*, New York, NY: UNICEF.

UNICEF (2002a) *Progress since the World Summit for Children: A statistical review*, New York, NY: UNICEF.

UNICEF (2002b) *The state of the world's children 2002*, New York, NY: UNICEF (also *Official Summary* at www.unicef.org/sowc02summary/).

UNICEF (2002c) *End decade assessment – MICS 2*, available at www.childinfo.org/MICS2/ Gj99306m.htm

UNICEF Innocenti Research Centre (2000) *Innocenti Report Card No 1, A league table of child poverty in rich nations*, Florence, Italy: UN Children's Fund, download free at www.unicef-icdc.org/cgi-bin/unicef Lunga.sql?ProductID=226

Vandemoortele, J. (2000) *Absorbing social shocks, protecting children and reducing poverty: The role of basic social services*, UNICEF Working Papers, New York, NY, UNICEF..

Vandemoortele, J. (2002) *Are the MDGs feasible?*, New York, NY: UN Development Programme Bureau for Development Policy.

WHO (World Health Organisation) (2001) *Macroeconomics and health: Investing in health for economic development, Report of the Commission on Macroeconomics and Health*, Geneva: WHO Publications.

WHO, UNICEF, WSSCC (2000) *The global water supply and sanitation assessment*, Geneva: WHO Publications.

World Bank (1990) *World Development Report 1990: Poverty*, Washington, DC: World Bank.

Appendix: Severe deprivation and absolute poverty among children: country data

State	Child (<18) population (000s) (2000)	% water deprived	% sanitation deprived	% shelter deprived	% information deprived	% education deprived	% food deprived	% health deprived	% severely deprived	% in absolute poverty	% urban children absolute poverty	% rural children absolute poverty
Bolivia	3,830	14.8	37.1	43.9	13.1	1.3	9.2	9.5	58.9	32.9	11.7	64.9
Brazil	59,515	–	15.0	11.8	8.3	2.4	2.7	5.5	25.3	10.0	4.3	27.7
Colombia	16,302	9.1	11.0	11.9	4.0	2.0	3.0	5.8	24.4	10.5	2.0	28.5
Dominican Republic	3,359	23.0	11.1	17.1	8.1	4.2	2.9	3.4	40.7	15.2	4.3	30.2
Guatemala	5,764	12.3	15.9	58.7	14.4	11.4	19.3	8.0	63.8	33.7	16.6	44.1
Haiti	3,915	42.6	44.9	49.8	41.6	18.2	16.2	25.5	74.6	56.6	15.8	77.7
Nicaragua	2,533	12.0	16.9	62.6	15.6	11.0	8.8	3.2	67.2	30.8	11.9	54.4
Peru	10,198	22.9	25.6	56.1	7.9	0.9	7.4	5.7	62.0	35.4	11.9	66.2
Egypt	28,663	8.3	6.2	41.9	27.6	11.3	14.0	8.0	56.7	26.6	8.5	38.9
Morocco	12,302	37.1	43.5	40.7	14.4	34.6	9.0	10.3	64.0	47.0	7.2	72.3
Yemen	10,295	49.8	58.9	59.1	19.0	36.3	6.5	45.6	86.6	67.6	17.8	78.5
Cambodia	6,832	59.1	80.8	8.6	37.6	17.3	12.1	29.2	91.8	70.8	8.0	92.0
China	378,939	3.7	1.7	3.0	3.3	0.3	4.5	0.3	13.1	1.6	1.8	1.5
Indonesia	78,233	24.0	15.6	21.7	21.1	2.6	–	9.8	51.2	19.8	5.3	27.3
Philippines	33,835	18.7	15.6	23.9	11.9	2.7	–	11.2	46.7	19.8	7.5	30.2
Bangladesh	62,494	2.5	24.6	89.7	47.4	19.7	30.2	16.5	92.5	62.4	24.9	66.6
India	399,798	19.4	68.3	36.8	38.3	15.6	26.3	21.4	79.9	57.2	21.2	68.4
Nepal	10,921	37.0	85.1	93.9	41.6	28.7	27.4	32.6	98.3	90.3	52.5	93.2
Pakistan	68,231	19.5	51.0	46.7	45.3	38.4	22.9	33.5	83.0	61.0	25.0	77.1
Benin	3,360	29.2	74.5	49.7	65.7	47.7	13.0	19.1	92.6	74.7	48.0	89.4
Burkina Faso	6,457	46.6	78.2	75.8	48.9	67.6	16.4	18.8	93.4	84.0	18.6	93.0
Cameroon	7,453	53.1	10.3	57.9	29.7	16.4	12.3	20.0	77.4	54.3	17.3	70.6

State	Child (<18) population (000s) (2000)	% water deprived	% sanitation deprived	% shelter deprived	% information deprived	% education deprived	% food deprived	% health deprived	% severely deprived	% in absolute poverty	% urban children absolute poverty	% rural children absolute poverty
Central African Republic	1,844	51.9	24.0	80.7	30.7	30.7	18.9	24.2	88.9	65.4	39.2	85.6
Chad	4,172	55.2	72.1	95.9	54.0	59.1	23.3	51.2	97.3	88.2	54.5	97.7
Comoros	355	51.8	0.3	55.3	42.8	35.4	14.1	13.6	87.5	56.5	33.0	64.8
Côte d'Ivoire	7,943	21.1	42.2	30.2	37.3	40.7	13.0	26.4	72.0	47.3	13.7	66.4
Ethiopia	32,456	74.9	83.9	95.1	56.5	61.1	28.5	32.3	97.8	94.0	58.6	99.2
Ghana	9,303	50.8	25.6	29.1	37.4	14.8	10.8	10.3	77.7	47.0	18.7	58.1
Guinea	4,145	44.4	43.5	57.0	48.1	55.7	8.9	25.9	87.9	71.1	31.5	86.7
Kenya	15,705	63.1	17.1	74.0	29.3	6.0	13.6	41.3	86.8	65.8	19.8	73.7
Madagascar	8,174	70.8	63.0	38.6	43.1	24.8	25.2	24.0	89.7	74.2	45.7	82.5
Malawi	6,002	52.8	24.9	85.1	42.6	30.1	22.6	9.9	91.6	74.6	28.9	80.9
Mali	5,980	18.8	26.7	79.3	31.3	67.9	26.2	33.1	87.2	63.5	26.8	77.3
Mauritania	1,353	37.5	51.6	77.1	44.2	19.7	17.8	22.3	90.1	70.5	47.4	85.9
Mozambique	9,231	56.7	59.7	74.7	45.6	28.0	17.9	29.1	89.7	76.3	37.8	87.5
Namibia	884	46.2	67.6	71.9	19.0	6.6	8.9	9.4	80.9	69.8	12.3	89.8
Niger	6,123	37.1	79.8	85.3	42.8	69.2	30.0	46.3	91.8	85.2	31.9	97.
Nigeria	59,108	44.0	26.0	45.1	35.4	22.1	16.0	39.7	78.8	52.6	22.1	64.5
Rwanda	3,941	88.7	5.8	89.2	39.4	23.9	20.5	9.2	97.3	86.9	39.2	89.3
Senegal	4,804	23.1	33.3	45.8	22.4	—	—	—	63.1	39.4	9.0	55.9
South Africa	17,589	28.5	16.2	25.8	12.9	2.1	—	3.5	45.5	24.3	3.9	42.2
Tanzania	18,258	67.0	13.3	83.2	49.8	34.9	18.3	20.4	91.9	78.1	36.1	88.5
Togo	2,310	31.4	66.9	33.3	45.5	21.1	12.0	19.4	83.5	61.9	23.4	73.0
Uganda	13,062	87.2	16.8	87.7	38.6	17.0	16.6	22.0	96.7	85.4	39.7	91.1
Zambia	5,571	45.8	26.9	59.8	34.2	20.1	18.1	7.3	75.6	56.8	17.9	81.9
Zimbabwe	6,645	41.5	31.9	34.8	31.1	5.2	9.7	11.9	66.7	45.3	1.0	60.8

Note: Percentages for food deprivation are for the population aged <5; percentages for education deprivation are for the population aged 7-18.